Women & Flowers

BY WELLERAN POLTARNEES

BLUE LANTERN BOOKS
1993

COPYRIGHT © 1993, BLUE LANTERN BOOKS. ALL RIGHTS RESERVED.
FIRST PRINTING. PRINTED IN HONG KONG.
ISBN 0-9621131-7-4

PREFACE

I am attracted by subjects to which there are no maps, no detailed accounts by those who have gone before. You would not think that women and flowers would pose such a challenge. The two components are familiar and exhaustively analyzed. Together, they are unexplored. I found books on woman gardeners, flower painters, collectors, arrangers, and books about woman as the mother of all creation, but my particular curiosity was not addressed. Why do we join women and flowers? Wherein lies their points of similarity and dissimilarity? Is there something more to the fact that artists so frequently picture them together than that they are both attractive subjects? If this is all there is to it, then why aren't women and birds, or women and oriental carpets, or women and trees nearly as common? I believe that to many observers there is an affinity between the two, and I have compiled this book to investigate the reasons for that perception.

Because I go into an uncharted place, because I find no books and only a few essays which touch directly on my area of inquiry, you will have to forgive the thoroughly speculative nature of this work. I am like a navigator travelling up a tropical river. I am surrounded by my subject, and can see many details, but I lack the perspective for an overview. I am dazzled by the colors, overwhelmed by the scent, intimidated by the abundance and variety of evidence. I send these notes back in the hope others will make the journey, and building upon my insights, discover more about this mysterious affinity. —W.P.

Woman as the Source of Flowers

The Great Mother occurs worldwide, under a variety of names and guises, as the creative force of nature. She is loved for her fecundity, her generosity, her motherhood, her endless bounty. She is the birth giver, the bringer of Spring.

*Hail, o greenest branch,
sprung forth in the airy breezes
of the prayers of the saints*

*So the time has come
that your sprays have flourished;
hail, hail to you,
because the heat of the sun has exuded from you
like the aroma of balm.*

*For the beautiful flower sprang from you
which gave all parched perfumes their aroma*

*And they have radiated anew
in their full freshness.*

—Hildegard of Bingen

WOMAN AS THE SOURCE OF FLOWERS

Woman as Flower

The comparison of women and flowers is almost as old as poetry itself, and occurs in the Occident, the Near East and the Far East. Since poets are merely humans with the gift of speaking rhythmically and concisely, then we may assume that mankind sees the matter as poets have.

Go, lovely Rose,
Tell her that wastes her time and me,
That now she knows,
When I resemble her to thee,
How sweet and fair she seems to be.
—Edmund Waller

Oh, my luve's like a red, red rose,
That's newly sprung in June:
Oh, my luve's like the melodie
That's sweetly played in tune.
—Robert Burns

There is a Garden in her face
Where Roses and white Lilies blow
—Thomas Campion

And yet your mouth, dear child,
Your mouth, dear child, is envied of the bees.
—from A Thousand and One Nights

Won't you come into the garden? I would like my roses to see you.
—Richard B. Sheridan

Her cheek had the pale pearly pink
Of sea shells, the world's sweetest tint, as though
She lived, one half might deem, on roses sopp'd
In pearly dew.
—Phillip Bailey

WOMAN AS FLOWER

Aside from the effulgent praise that poets pour forth when talking of women and flowers there are numerous other points of likeness defined, both by men and women, both in verse and prose.

Their gowns dazzled with gold and silver; out of monstrous farthingales their slender forms rose like the stems of flowers.
—Alexander Pushkin

*I walk down the garden-paths,
And all the daffodils
Are blowing, and the bright blue squills.
I walk down the patterned garden-paths
In my stiff, brocaded gown.
With my powdered hair and jeweled fan,
I too am a rare
Pattern. As I wander down
The garden-Paths.*
—Amy Lowell

*Indolent! indolent!—Yes I am indolent!
So is the grass growing tenderly, slowly:
So is the violet fragrant and lowly.
Drinking in quietness, peace, and content:*
—Rose Terry Cooke

...he said I was a flower of the mountain yes so we are flowers all a woman's body yes that was one true thing he said in his life and the sun shines for you today yes that was why I like him because I saw he understood or felt what a woman is...
—James Joyce

WOMAN AS FLOWER

FLOWER AS WOMAN

𝒫ersonification is the attribution of human form or character to objects. It occurs frequently in poetry and in art. The authors and illustrators of children's books are particularly fond of personification, as they believe children prefer this view of existence. It is true that in ancient times, the childhood of civilization, personification abounded. Life, Death, Earth, Ocean, Sky, Weather, Good and Bad Fortune, Justice, Victory, and so on, were understood to have human character and form. Primitive societies also see us as living in a world of presences with traits very much like our own. Science and cosmology have eroded our tendency to personify, at least in public view, but it remains a very natural way of understanding.

FLOWER AS WOMAN

Flowers are most frequently personified as women. Children are also common, but male flowers are rare. When seen as male they are almost always spiky, thorny, or inconspicuous plants such as thistle, ragwort, ot wild thyme. Roses, lilies, tulips, violets—all of the most popular and decorative flowers are almost invariably female.

The reason that flowers are seen as women is the thesis of this book. Flowers and women are linked creatures. Claude Bragdon, in his philosophic speculation Delphic Woman, says of woman, "she it is that forces the thorny stalk of life to put forth blossoms," and, "she fecundates man's imagination and inspires him to endeavor through her beauty, her mystery, and miracle of her tenderness." He, like most of us, has thoroughly confused woman and flowers.

FLOWER AS WOMAN

In personifying an object one is not forced to select a sex. An artist simply needs to add eyes, arms, and legs to have a flower person without gender. Most visual personifications are sexless. Shovels, buckets, airplanes, clocks, books— these seldom are men or women. The fact that flowers are predominantly female demonstrates further a powerful tendency to equate woman and flower. The traits that flowers most clearly share with women are, beauty, grace of form, colorful and elaborate adornment, evanescence, a sweet odor, and apparent delicacy.

Walter Crane (1845-1915), the great English designer and book illustrator, returned in book after book to flower people. He had the gift of giving the flowers the human form that perfectly expressed their character as flowers.

Grandville (1803-1847)brought his unique vision to focus in Les Fleurs Animées(1847). Unlike Crane he was less interested in finding the proper human form for each type of flower, but rather satirized humankind by showing how like flowers the various types of people were. Despite this difference of emphasis his work is equally attractive and convincing.

FLOWER AS WOMAN

The slender acacia would not shake
   One long milk-bloom on the tree;
The white lake-blossom fell into the lake,
   As the pimpernel dozed on the lea;
But the rose was awake all night for your sake,
   Knowing your promise to me;
The lilies and roses were all awake,
   They sighed for the dawn and thee.

Queen rose of the rosebud garden of girls,
   Come hither, the dances are done,
In gloss of satin and glimmer of pearls,
   Queen lily and rose in one;
Shine out, little head, sunning over with curls.
   To the flowers, and be their sun.

There has fallen a splendid tear
   From the passion-flower at the gate.
She is coming, my dove, my dear;
   She is coming, my life, my fate;
The red rose cries, "She is near, she is near;"
   And the white rose weeps, "She is late;"
The larkspur listens, "I hear, I hear;"
   And the lily whispers, "I wait."

She is coming, my own my sweet;
   Were it ever so airy a tread,
My heart would hear her and beat,
   Were it earth in an earthy bed;
My dust would hear her and beat,
   Had I lain for a century dead;
Would start and tremble under her feet,
   And blossom in purple and red.
                        —Alfred, Lord Tennyson

"O Tiger-lily," said Alice, addressing herself to one that was waving gracefully about in the wind, "I wish you could talk!" "We can talk," said the Tiger-lily: "when there's anybody worth talking to."
                        —Lewis Carroll

Women Enjoying Flowers

...What happiness to sit on this tufty knoll and fill my basket with the blossoms! What a renewal of heart and mind! To inhabit such a scene of peace and sweetness is again to be fearless, gay and gentle as a child. Then it is that thought becomes poetry and feeling religion. Then it is that we are happy and good.
—Mary Russell Mitford

All of us enjoy flowers. Women have had, historically, more leisure to grow, tend, cut, arrange, and contemplate them. Many believe that women enjoy them more because of some deep, instinctive affinity.

WOMEN ENJOYING FLOWERS

WOMEN ENJOYING FLOWERS

A great part of the beauty of Mrs. Thaxter's house in the Isles of Shoals was made up of flowers. I have never anywhere seen such realized possibilities of color! The fine harmonic sense of the woman and artist and poet thrilled through these long chords of color, and filled the room with an atmosphere which made it seem like living in a rainbow.

—Candace Wheeler

The kinship of beauty is certainly one of the reasons that women enjoy flowers. Another is the sensual pleasure found in the form, color, texture and scent of flowers. Man observing this enjoyment is made to realize that she is a being with deep sensate needs, and feels thereby assured that he, in some small way, might be allowed entry to that dimension of her being.

The arts of dress and personal adornment have been more the domain of woman than of man, at least since the beginning of the 19th century. The decoration of homes has likewise been, primarily, woman's responsibility. Flowers being an important part of both of these areas, it is natural that they should spend much time together.

WOMEN ENJOYING FLOWERS

Women Offering Flowers

The essential power of women offering flowers comes from two assumptions. First, that women are themselves, in some sense, flowers. Though this is more prevalently a man's than a woman's view, most women accept the comparison. Second, that in offering anything one offers some portion of themselves, and the more kinship between the offerer and the thing offered the more personal the gift.

Regardless of how many or how few different books a woman might have, she would certainly have the one item owned by nearly everyone-- that is, a volume containing a list of the language of flowers. The Victorians found the idea irresistible and the floral sentiments exactly right for their gentle and unworldly age.
— Doris Swarthout

Almond, Flowering	Hope
Anemone	Forsaken
Bell Flower	Constancy
Cherry Blossom	Spiritual Beauty
Clematis	Mental Beauty
Coreopsis	Always Cheerful
Crocus	I Am His
Daisy	Innocence
Everlasting	Always Remembered
Flower Of An Hour	Delicate Beauty
Forget-Me-Not	True Love
Heliotrope	Devotion
Honeysuckle	Fidelity
Jonquil	Is My Affection Returned?
Ladies Delight	Forget Me Not
Lily Of The Valley	Unnoticed Affection
Lily, White	Purity And Modesty
Love In A Mist	Perplexity
Mimosa	Sensitiveness
Nightshade	Dark Thoughts
Orange Blossom	Woman's Worth
Petunia	Elegance Without Pride
Phlox	Our Souls Are United
Pink, Red	Woman's Love
Rose, Bridal	Happy Love
Rose, Musk	Charming
Rosebud, Moss	Confession of Love
Rosebud, White	Too Young To Love
Snapdragon	Dazzling, But Dangerous
Tulip, Red	Declaration of Love
Violet, Blue	Faithfulness
Violet, White	Modesty

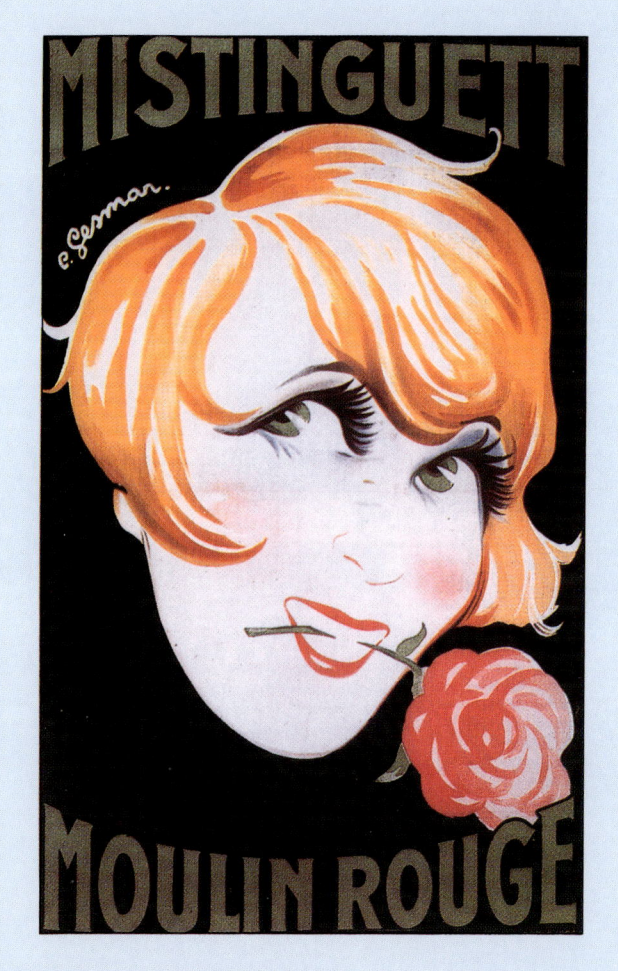

Woman Conscious of Her Likeness to Flowers

Most women leave it to men to see them as flowers. They are themselves too aware of their own complexity, their own imperfection, to see their likeness to anything as simple and flawless as a flower.

Occasionally women do see their kinship with flowers, and are glad to have it so. The woman to the left is one of these. She feels herself on equal footing with their glory.

They throw their color like a shawl
About me. I am proud and tall
And pledged to bravery, since came
Delphiniums
                — Anne Lloyd

The woman to the lower right is conscious of the gentler aspects of the floral comparison, and is pleased.

After long dreaming in the folded bud,
    After long nights of waiting—ah, who
        knows
How joyous a surprise, to open wide
    And find one's self—a rose!
              — May Lewis

WOMAN CONSCIOUS OF HER LIKENESS TO FLOWERS

Women Nurturing Flowers

*I*nasmuch as woman is mother, the giver of life, then flowers are properly in her care. Because of their beauty and apparent fragility they are especially appropriate subjects for her attention.

In the 19th century many women were freed from housekeeping by inexpensive servants, and turned to a variety of hobbies, gardening being one of the favorites.

As orchards to men, so are flowers and herbs to women. Indeed the garden appears celibate, as does the house, without womanly hands to plant and care for it.
—*Amos Bronson Alcott*

The cultivation of Annual Flowers is a delightful employment, and well adapted to the amusement of a lady, who, with the assistance of a laborer to prepare the ground, may turn a barren waste into a beauteous flower garden with her own hands. Sowing the seed, transplanting, watering, and training the plants, tying them to sticks as props, leading them over trellis-work, and gathering their seed, are all suitable feminine occupations, and from their affording motives for exercise in the open air, they contribute greatly to health and tranquillity of mind.
—*Thomas Bridgeman*

My
Love to you.
Dear Valentine,
I send you here
Love and devotion
from a heart
sincere.

Woman Thinking About Flowers

Philosophers belie that the universe can best be understood by studying small and comprehensible parts. Flowers have been a favorite area of inquiry because though they reveal no more truth than a flea, the research offers more delight.

To see a world in a grain of sand
And a heaven in a wild flower,
Hold infinity in the palm of your hand
And eternity in an hour.
—William Blake

Flower in the crannied wall,
I pluck you out of the crannies,
I hold you here, root and all, in my hand,
Little flower but if I could understand
What you are, root and all, and all in all,
I should know what God and man is.
—Alfred, Lord Tennyson

WOMEN THINKING ABOUT FLOWERS

The eighteenth century organized humankind's passion for flowers. Plant classification was refined. Species were imported and exported worldwide (nine thousand new plants were imported into Britain). Flower painting flourished. Elaborate gardens were planned and accomplished.

In the nineteenth century interest in flowers spread from a small body of enthusiasts to the population as a whole. Almost every home had a garden, and the entire household was involved in its maintenance. Popular editions of books on flowers and gardening sold by the tens of thousands. Albums of pressed flowers abounded. Indoor plants were almost universal, and larger homes had solaria. Flower gardening was an almost universal preoccupation.

The prevailing Victorian view was that the study of nature revealed the perfection and magnificence of God's design for creation. Close observation of nature's parts therefore tended to expand one's sense of wonder, and deepen one's faith.

WOMEN ARRANGING FLOWERS

To arrange flowers is to create a small universe according to one's own laws. The flowers can be tall or short as one wills, their leaves and foliage as varied as one desires.

Even more than gardening, flower arranging is the domain of woman. In the nineteenth century a body of skills developed that were required of every woman aspiring to be cultured. They included playing the piano, singing, one or more needlecrafts, and a variety of flower arts, including flower arranging.

Every housewife, at that time, was expected to add grace and beauty to her home. Flowers are, of course, one of the best means to these ends. Homes would feature one or more flower arrangements (in winter constructed of dried plants). Fresh nosegays were frequently made and given. Dinner parties demanded elaborate table arrangements, and hostesses were judged by the originality and profusion of their displays. Church altars frequently included flowers, and the women of the altar guild were expected to decorate weekly.

WOMEN ARRANGING FLOWERS

WOMEN & FLOWERS AS ATTRACTIVE COMPANIONS

I must admit that an artist need not have a deep motive in combining attractive objects in a picture. If the challenge is to achieve an attractive portrait of a woman, why not have her sit or stand near to flowers, particularly if they are found in the room? Am I not studying too hard to find significance in this choice? Perhaps, but why so often flowers, and so infrequently walls of books, tapestries or cats?

Methinks a being that is beautiful becometh more so as it looks on beauty, the eternal beauty of undying things.

—Lord Byron

WOMEN & FLOWERS AS ATTRACTIVE COMPANIONS

Women & Flowers: Two of the Chief Beauties of Creation

My search for scholarship or speculation on woman and flowers was, as I said in the preface, largely blossomless. The best articulation of the common view that I discovered was in an 1871 volume, *Salad for the Solitary*. There, in an essay titled "Facts and Fancies about Flowers," I found the summary which is quoted in full on the facing page.

The two divinest things this world has got,
A lovely woman in a rural spot!
—Leigh Hunt

WOMEN & FLOWERS: TWO OF THE CHIEF BEAUTIES OF CREATION

Woman, from her finer sensibilities and keener appreciation of the beautiful, possesses an innate passion for buds and blossoms, and these emblems of innocence, grace, and beauty naturally enlist her sympathies. She is indeed, herself, the queenly blossom of Paradise, and her peerless charms find their nearest emblems in the blushing tints, the nectar sweets, and glowing beauties of Flora. Hence the fitting grace with which she prefers to cull from the leafy temple of the goddess, the rarest gems to heighten her fascinations, rather than costly pearls or the dazzling decorations of art.
—Frederick Saunders

WOMEN & FLOWERS: TWO OF THE CHIEF BEAUTIES OF CREATION

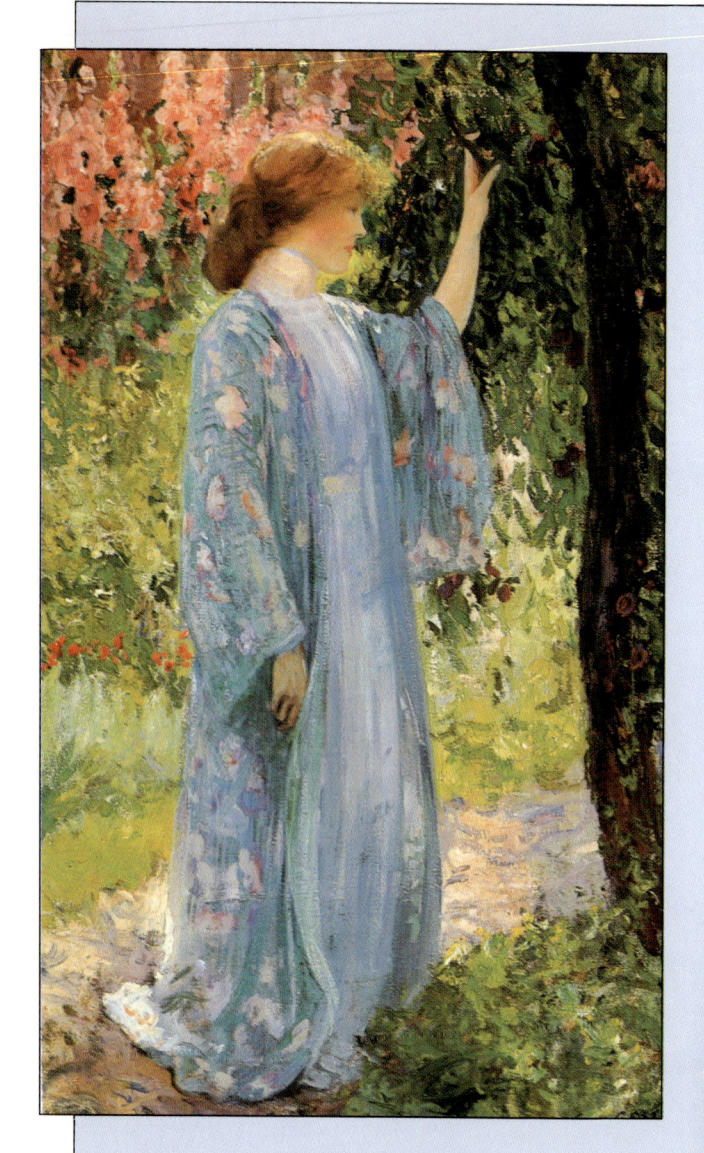

Kant says, "the beautiful is that which is an object of universal delight." Though there is no absolutely universal concord on the beautiful, there is more agreement on the attractions of flowers and women than on almost any other aspects of creation. It is true that there are no universal standards of feminine beauty— one prefers dark, another light, one tall, another short— but when an exceptionally attractive woman appears there is little disagreement, most observers admitting that she has attained to beauty, even though she may not be to their particular taste. With flowers there is even more unanimity. Though one may prefer lilies to tulips, most will admit that flowers possess unique and remarkable beauty. Thus flowers and women live together on a plane above.

The straight line makes a lesser claim upon our artistic sensibilities than the curved. Certainly the Pyramids of Egypt are compelling, but beauty may not best describe their achievement. If one compares the Empire State Building and The Chrysler Building, there is no doubt which is the more beautiful. The former depends upon straight lines for its effect, the latter upon curves, and the curves triumph.

Flowers and women are concatenations of curves and prove the truth of Bulwer-Lytton's assertion, "In life, as in art, the beautiful moves in curves."

WOMEN & FLOWERS: TWO OF THE CHIEF BEAUTIES OF CREATION

For the eye is quick, and seems to have been more docile to the education of life than the heart or the reason of man, and able sooner to adapt itself to the reality. Beauty therefore seems to be the clearest manifestation of perfection, and the best evidence of its possibility. If perfection is, as it should be, the ultimate justification of being, we may understand the ground of the moral diginity of beauty. Beauty is a pledge of the possible conformity between the soul and nature, and consequently a ground of faith in the supremacy of the good.

—George Santayana

There is a deep current of belief (with its origin in the medieval court of love) that woman is the pinnacle of God's achievement. As a Victorian writer put it, "...she is the most lovely of all created creatures. Her beauty is an influence which spreads beyond her person, and, like the sunshine, carries brightness into dark places."

Flowers, also, have been widely considered to be one of the loveliest of all aspects of creation. Edmund Burke in his Inquiry Into the Sublime and Beautiful, says, "Turning our eyes to the vegetable creation, we find there nothing so beautiful as flowers." Louisa Twamley writes, "I love flowers, as forming one of the sweetest lines in the Poem of Nature; a universal blessing accessible to all natures, climes and classes."

Occupying as they do the same peak of excellence it is natural that women and flowers should get to know each other well, and be closely associated in our minds.

31

Women Exulting in Flowers

To exult is to surrender to joy. We give way to exultation either when a good surprises us, or when a good is so powerful that it breaks down our ordinary defenses and reveals us unmasked.

WOMEN EXULTING IN FLOWERS

WOMEN EXULTING IN FLOWERS

WOMEN EXULTING IN FLOWERS

I think I am quite wicked with roses. I like to gather them, and smell them till they have no scent left.

—*George Eliot*

Oh, I love the flowers! Other people exclaim over them and say, 'Aren't they lovely?' but I feel about them differently, and the flowers know that I love them.

—*Celia Thaxter*

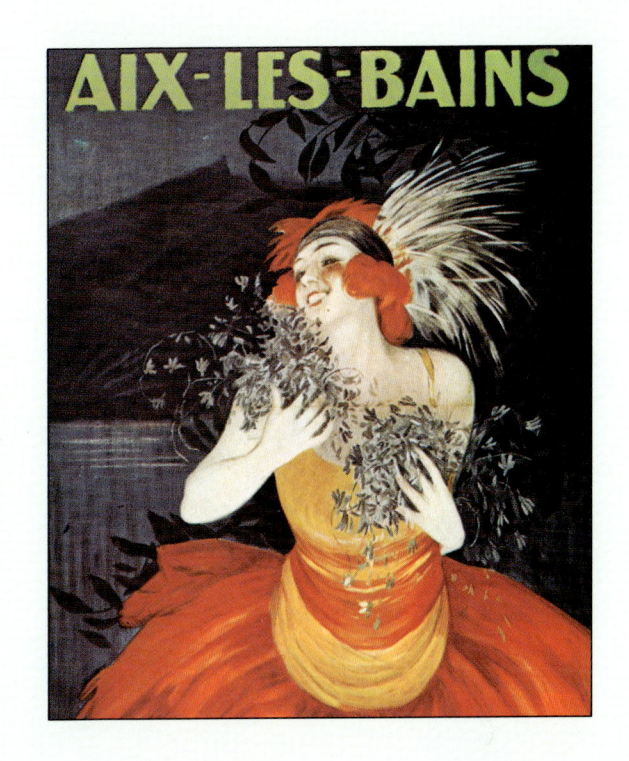

Women Receiving Flowers

No gift is more often given to women than flowers. All classes and conditions of men from a laborer returning from the fields with a small nosegay for his wife, to an eighteenth century courtier presenting a bouquet and a verse to a lady, recognize the simple rightness of this gift. Both sexes know that it is the gift of all gifts, not to be measured by cost or rarity, and that it carries with it a meaning and message beyond words.

WOMEN RECEIVING FLOWERS

Usually the gift of flowers to women is made when there is a romantic dimension to the relations between the giver and receiver. This is, however, not the sole grounds of rightness for this gift to a woman. From a child the gift says, I am simple and you are good. From another woman it says, you and I and the flowers share a great deal. To an elderly woman the gift says, your feminity is not gone or forgotten.

THIS BOOK WAS SET IN GARAMOND, TRAJAN AND CATHEDRAL BY
THE BLUE LANTERN STUDIO.

PICTURE CREDITS

FRONT COVER
    RHYS, DYNEVOR. MAGAZINE COVER, 1936

TITLE PAGE
    MARTY. *GAZETTE DE BON TON*, 1920

COPYRIGHT PAGE
    PRESSLER, GENE. "MARY PICKFORD," 1923

PAGE

1   ANONYMOUS. FRENCH POSTCARD, N.D.
2   MARTIN, RENÉ. ADVERTISING ART, 1935
3   BESKOW, ELSA. *BLOMSTERFESTEN*, N.D.
4   MUCHA, ALPHONSE. "PRINTEMPS," 1900
5   ANONYMOUS. FASHION PLATE, N.D.
6   LEFT: KIESEL, CONRAD. "AT THE WINDOW," N.D. • RIGHT: ANONYMOUS.
7   BOSTON, F. "IN LOTUS LAND," 1900
8   KREIDOLF, ERNST. *DER TRAUMGARTEN*, N.D.
9   HERFORD, OLIVER. "THE LAST ROSE," 1923
10   LEFT: CRANE, WALTER. *A FLOWER WEDDING*, 1905 • RIGHT: GRANDVILLE, J.J. *LES FLEURS ANIMÉES*, 1847
11   DE MORGAN, EVELYN. "CLYTIE," 1887
12   TOP: ANONYMOUS. VICTORIAN SCRAP, N.D. • BOTTOM: HASSAM, FREDERICK CHILDE. "SUMMER EVENING," 1886
13   PACKER, FRED L. ADVERTISING ART, 1920
14   TOP: KAY, GERTRUDE A. *SOME POEMS OF CHILDHOOD*, 1931 • BOTTOM: CLAPSADDLE, ELLEN. POSTCARD, 1912
15   ALMA-TADEMA, SIR LAWRENCE. "WOMAN AND FLOWERS," 1868
16   TOP: SEIFERT, ALFRED. CALENDAR ART, N.D. • BOTTOM: ANONYMOUS. NEW YEARS CARD, N.D.
17   TOP: CZACHORSKI, LADISLAS VON. "AN ITALIAN BEAUTY," N.D. BOTTOM: GESMAR, CHARLES. POSTER, 1926
18   TOP: ANONYMOUS. POSTCARD, 1909 • BOTTOM: BENDA, W.T. MAGAZINE COVER, 1924
19   PHILLIPS, COLES. ADVERTISING ART, N.D.
20   TOP: LORD, CAROLINE. "WOMAN WITH A GERANIUM," N.D.
    BOTTOM: BRICKDALE, ELEANOR FORTESCUE. *GOLDEN BOOK OF FAMOUS WOMEN*, N.D.
21   ANONYMOUS. VALENTINE, N.D.
22   TOP: WINTER, CHARLES A. BOOK ILLUSTRATION, 1910 • BOTTOM: EVANS, DE SCOTT. "BOTANIZING," 1891
23   CURRAN, CHARLES. "CHRYSANTHEMUMS," 1890
24   TOP: PHILLIPS, COLES. MAGAZINE COVER, 1911 • BOTTOM: MOLL, CARL. "BEI DER ANRICHTE," 1903
25   LEWIS, JOHN FREDERICK. "IN THE BEY'S GARDEN," N.D.
26   TOP: BERTHON, PAUL. "LES CHRYSANTHEMES," 1899 • BOTTOM: ANONYMOUS. CALENDAR ART, N.D.
27   BEATON, CECIL. "MARLENE DIETRICH," 1932
28   TOP: VILA, EMILIO. POSTER, 1935 • BOTTOM: KILBURNE, GEORGE. "PENNING A LETTER," N.D.
29   CURRAN, CHARLES. MAGAZINE COVER, 1916
30   TOP: ROSE, GUY. "THE BLUE KIMONO", 1909 • BOTTOM: VERNON, EMIL. "THE FANCY BONNET," N.D.
31   TOP: GEVORSS."GLAMOROUS", N.D. • BOTTOM: LARSSON, CARL. "EIGHTEEN YEARS OLD," 1902
32   TOP: MARTY. FASHION PLATE, 1921 • BOTTOM: ALMA-TADEMA, SIR LAWRENCE. "SUMMER OFFERING," 1911
33   LEPAPE. MAGAZINE COVER, 1919
34   ANONYMOUS. PERFUME ADVERTISEMENT, N.D.
35   TOP: CAPPIELLO. POSTER, 1921 • BOTTOM: BOILEAU PHILIP. POSTCARD, 1905
36   TOP: ANONYMOUS. VICTORIAN PAINTING, N.D. • BOTTOM: ANONYMOUS, MAGAZINE ADVERTISEMENT, 1925
37   TOP: ANONYMOUS. MAGAZINE ILLUSTRATION, 1921
    CENTER: LEVOIVENEL, GEORGES. FLORIST'S ADVERTISEMENT,1932
    BOTTOM: ANONYMOUS. MAGAZINE ADVERTISEMENT, 1922
38   TISSOT, JACQUES JOSEPH. "THE LITTLE BUNCH OF LILACS," 1875

BACK COVER
    KHNOPFF, FERNAND, "BROWN EYES AND ONE BLUE FLOWER," 1905